ENVELOPES

KEVIN PETERSON

I dedicate this collection of poems to my Dear Grandfather, Late Dr. Krishna Prasad Deo, Principal, A.S College, Satsang, Deoghar. I have inherited this talent from him, as he himself has a series of books published in philosophy, which has been enlightening the students at college level. I would equally give the credit of acquiring this talent from my Dear Papa, who has written many articles in National Newspaper, Dainik Bhaskar. My mother and maternal grandfather have also been a source of inspiration for me

Contents

Acknowledgements

Firstly, I want to thank Alex Alfred Soy who helped me in few of my poems, the description of this book and gave some ideas regarding the title. I am thankful to all those who supported and motivated me to publish this book. The credits for the book cover goes to the respective artist. At last I want to thank my friend Luna who unknowingly inspired me to write my first poem.

1. The Smile

After getting ahold of myself,
I finally moved on,
I started living a simple life again,
Finally there was no pain,
Moon and stars seemed brighter than before,
I wasn't sad anymore,

I gained my health back to how it was,
My body perished all the scars.
I decided not to fall in love again,
As I was afraid to endure that pain,
But then you smiled.

2. Empty Birthday

The clock has hit midnight,
You are not the first one to wish this time,
Neither you are the last,
The whole day has passed.

The one thing I missed the most this birthday,
Was your video call, but now you have moved far away.
How the times have passed,
I don't even know if our memories will last.

There is nothing special about this day anymore,
Birthday used to feel differently before.
But I not sad, neither I am happy,
It feels just like a normal day but a bit empty.

Enter Caption

3. Machine with Blood and Skin

Why is this happening again?
I tried my best and still I am in pain,
All the sleepless nights are now in vain,
I am just lying on my bed, my eyes are strained.

I feel a void inside me,
This unknown pain is penentrating deep,
Still I am not able to weep,
I am so tired but not able to fall asleep.

This is not the first time I failed,
I've tried again and again,
But results are always the same,
It is driving me insane.

Now I am giving up on my dream,
I am giving up on my god, and everything.
I'll just drown in the ocean of failure,
Maybe I am a misfit in this nature.

What has happened to me?
I don't feel a thing,

Am I just a machine with blood and skin?
Why do I always lose and never win?

4. What If

I am sitting alone in my chamber,
Trying hard to remember,
What if I never moved out of my village,
My life would have painted a different image.

Should I've not taken that train,
Maybe I could've suffered less pain,
Maybe I would've traveled an infrequent venture,
But at least I could admire some adventures.

I wonder what would've happened if I stayed on my farm,
Working till dusk wouldn't be such harm.
Maybe then I wouldn't be required to drink,
And force myself to sleep.

I visualize what my life could be,
Where I was not forced by decree,
To the pleasures, I shouldn't have agreed,
At least then, I could live free.

5. Everytime

Every single night when I was not able to sleep,
Everytime I digged in way too deep,
Everytime I went through a hardship,
Everytime I sailed in a wrecked ship,
Every moment when I craved for a kiss,
Every inch of my body wanted that bliss,
Every Christmas the candles I lit,
Every winter the sweaters I knit,
Every crime that I ever commit,
Everything was for you,
But I guess it never mattered,
Isn't that right my love?

6. Love and Distress

My heart is feeling that sensation again,
The sensation which caused me pain,
Because of which my efforts went in vain,
And I ended up alone in the end.

I can't sleep as she is in my dreams,
I want her to know how much she means to me.
But I am afraid of being left alone,
I am afraid from skin to bone.

Whenever I see her, I ask myself,
Should I trust again?
Is there something I will gain?
Or like always will it go in vain?

Sometimes I think to confess,
But past memories put me in distress.
I want my heart to rest,
And my brain to take a break.

I have so many things to say,
I think I should wait,
Until she feels the same,

So that this time, my love won't go in vain.

7. Barren December

December doesn't feel like December,
It feels like a normal month this year,
Fog is hailing but my sight is clear,
I don't freeze in morning though summer isn't near.

Christmas is near,
Mistletoes have disappeared,
Thanksgiving is coming, there's no one to volunteer,
Last week of this year will go barren I fear.

I think I know why all this is happening,
Maybe I know why snow is not falling.
Last year I had my guard down,
I helped some comrades who are presently nonwhere to be found.

At the graveyard,
I remember giving a red rose to someone special,
I remember the aura, it was exceptional,
That individual knew many secrets which were personal,
That red rose was left abandoned there,
It was burning like an arsenal.

As I saw that red rose turn black,

I had a peculiar pain, almost like a heart attack.

As I healed, my emotions went away with that peculiar pain,

From that moment I knew, December will not feel like December again.

8. Lost Another Love

Another day, I lost another love,
But this time she was just a little dove.
I never realized when she was filled with so much hate,
I could've done something but it was too late.

24 hours a day, 21 hours I used to be alone,
Rest 3 hours I talked with her on phone.
Now I am blocked for exactly no reason,
I think she committed a treason.

She is really happy with her family and friends,
But I still remember our conversation which had no end.
I guess she don't even miss me,
But her picture is the biggest in my album, I guarantee.

Now my days are filled with monotone,
Every single second I am alone.
I guess evening walks were not enough,
It was just another day, I lost another love